PORTRAITS OF HOPE!

FINDING THE BRIGHT SIDE IN A DARK PLACE

by
Jacqueline Marie Sparaco

Imagination Press, LLC

Romans 8:32

Editors:
Doc Wilson
Teresa Hamilton

Layout Artist:
Doc Wilson

Illustrator:
CiCi Thacker

Graphic Artist:
Molly Sparaco Bowen

Portraits of Hope!

Finding the Bright Side In A Dark Place

First Edition

Printed in the United States of America

ISBN: 978-0-692-51618-8

Disclaimer

This book is based on true life events in the life of the author, Jacqueline Marie Sparaco. In some cases, names have been changed to protect the identity of certain individuals. Any similarities of events disclosed herein with those of any other person(s) are likely to be coincidental, and are expressly disavowed and disclaimed by the author and by the publishing company, Imagination Press, LLC.

Dedication

I would like to dedicate this book to:

My husband, Patrick, who has loved me over these 24+ years! Our 3 children: Sean, Molly, and Andrew . . . I love you "more than chocolate and bigger than the moon!" Always hope! My 8 siblings, my "forever friends": Sandy, Mike, Karen, Kathy, Dave, Jeff, Tim, and Cynthia. In loving memory of my mom, especially, for always believing in me. With special thanks to Rebecca Cymek, Pastor Greg and Peggy Carr, Pastor Steve and LaDon Hall, and Bishop William Newman for love, faith, and prayers. And to Loretta L. Shott – though now you are in heaven: you impressed upon me the need to publish my writings! To Terri and Brian Siwinski, and Maria Rivera . . . my dear, dear friends.

Thank you Teresa Hamilton and Doc Wilson for gifting me with this opportunity.

"You are the light of the world. A city set on a hill cannot be hidden; nor does anyone light a lamp and put it under a basket, but on the lamp stand, and it gives light to all who are in the house. 'Let your light shine before men in such a way that they may see your good works, and glorify your Father who is in heaven.' [Matthew 5:14-16.]"

Table of Contents

The Vessel

"Now in a great house there are not only vessels of gold and silver, but also of wood and clay, some for honorable use, some for dishonorable. Therefore, if anyone cleanses himself from what is dishonorable, he will be a vessel for honorable use, set apart as holy and useful to the master of the house, ready for every good work. [2 Timothy 2:20-21]"

It was only days ago when I found myself in the Valley of Decision. In my hands was a vessel – a water pitcher. This vessel had been with me my whole life. But now, I found myself despising this vessel. I reached a conclusion: This vessel was no longer favorable or useful. I found it to be rather undesirable and certainly not worth saving. After all, it was covered with cracks and it leaked. Its shell was faded. "Who in their right mind would hang onto this, let alone, drink from it!? How could something that wasn't yet old, be so damaged?" I asked myself. Its "aged appearance" seemed to boast of many travels, but, truthfully, it had barely travelled at all!

My dilemma? This was the only vessel I owned. I looked it over one last time. Then, raising it high above my head and closing my eyes, I cast it down! Somehow, as it released from my grip, someone else's hands grabbed mine and the vessel, saving it from certain disaster! I opened my eyes to see a stranger. As I glared at him, his eyes only returned a kind gaze. I was taken aback, startled. He spoke to me in a tender and kind voice as he began telling me of someone he knew, who restored "damaged" and broken vessels. (I felt sheepish and ashamed – hearing and knowing that my vessel was clearly both). He continued speaking, without pause, describing the Master Restorer. Then he showed me, with my own vessel, how it carried the Alpha and Omega Seal on the bottom. I had never even noticed the seal before!

He had my attention, but I was still somewhat skeptical. I lingered a little longer to hear more of what he had to say.

It was then that I learned this stranger's name. He was Menachem. (In Hebrew, this meant "Comforter.") His eyes blazed with excitement as he told me story after story of many people who had taken their broken vessels to the Master. Not one had lost its worth or value! This Master Restorer restored each and every one, miraculously! I found myself longing deeply to have what they had found. And yet, my water pot, in its condition, caused me much fear and doubt. Could it really, ever, be repaired or used again? I was ashamed and I hated it. It was so worthless!

Time passed by since my encounter with Menachem. He made it clear, though, that I could contact him if I had any more questions. Since then, a seed of faith sprouted in my heart, and was growing – faith that I had never experienced before. I thought more and more about taking the journey to the Master Restorer. Finally, when I could wait and wonder no longer, I started the journey. Following the directions Menachem had given me, I carefully travelled through field and valley, hill and road. It became clear to me when I was nearing his home because I recognized the landmarks I had been told to look for. An unusually large oak tree standing near a field, and a pond. Also, a little white bench and a drinking fountain. I had been told that the Master created the fountain and pond to refresh sojourners on their way to and from the area.

I had one more hill to climb. My feet felt heavier with each step. My heart was pounding hard in my chest. My palms were sweaty. I paused a moment to catch my breath. My thoughts were racing: "What if I am rejected again?" And "Could I handle that?" "Will He be like the others in my past who had seen my state and given up on me?" "Or worse, will He judge and declare my vessel condemned!?" The heat of the late afternoon sun was baking me as the harassing questions were filling me with fear. Yet, as soon as the questions came, they quickly quieted down within me. A powerful and very cool wind distracted me. I was soothed as it seemed to gently push me forward – as if something or someone was nudging me. My energy swiftly renewed, and peace came over me. I realized that I had to complete this journey. I had to take this chance.

THE MASTER'S HOME (The Vessel)

"The word which came to Jeremiah from the LORD saying 'Arise and go down to the potter's house, and there I will announce My words to you.' Then I went down to the potter's house, and there he was, making something on the wheel. But the vessel that he was making of clay was spoiled in the hands of the potter; so he remade it into another vessel, as it pleased the potter to make. [Jeremiah 18:1-4]"

Here I was – standing at the entrance of a lovely walkway to the Master's home. Myriads upon myriads of flowers lined the walkway. I recognized the scent of honeysuckle. There were also lilacs and rosebushes nearby. One of the floral vines that was so fragrant was wisteria growing along the fence posts and arbors. Even His doorway and window sills had fragrant and beautiful flowers and vines. "How beautiful!" I thought. The Master's home was so welcoming. The air around me felt light and soothing. I straightened my posture and knocked on the door. As the door swung open, I was greeted by the Man. He stood tall, ducking down a bit in the doorway, but He bid me to come in – all the while smiling. He looked so strong, having a solid and muscular stature. But His eyes were very gentle. It was clear that He had been expecting me. I felt very welcomed.

He led me toward two comfortable chairs by a warm, crackly fire – which I welcomed because it had begun to get chilly as the sun was setting low over the horizon. Light danced through the windows and onto the wall. Colors of amber and purple bounced off the glassware perched on His shelves. He continued to smile at me warmly. He offered me some hot tea to drink, which I accepted graciously. Then, we settled into our comfy seats.

It was quiet for only a minute or so, but it felt like an eternity! Our eyes met and, feeling self-conscious, my eyes sought refuge in the floor below. His gaze seemed to go through me to my very soul. Here I was, a woman fallen from grace and beauty. How could I be in the presence of this great Man? He cleared His throat and I looked back up, but instead of disdain, His eyes were warm and accepting. He gestured to me to hand the vessel over to Him. I surrendered it, feeling ashamed again about its condition. He raised it up, high in the air, and read out loud, "Fashioned for the Alpha and Omega." He followed this with "Hmm, uh huh," very approvingly. When next He spoke, His voice sounded like rushing water: it was powerful, but not scary. He said to me, "This is very good. Yes. Very good indeed." He turned it in His hands – looking closely, and then lifted it up higher in the air. He asked, "Have you ever heard about the great recall on these vessels? The one specifically for Alpha and Omega Vessels?" I responded shyly, "No. No, I have not." Then, He proceeded to explain. "Well, some time ago, a declaration went throughout all the country encouraging everyone to bring his or her vessel back to the Master for restoration. For, long, long ago, while the vessels were being created and formed, a rebellious worker began infiltrating the clay with a tainted substance. This substance compromised the integrity of every vessel. The ingredients of this tainted substance had impurities that were saturated with pride, rebellion, and even idolatry." I was shocked to learn of this tragic story, but I listened further as He continued. "So, when it was discovered, it was determined that every vessel was affected. Thus, the call went out for each vessel to be returned and restored by the True Master." He smiled at me again. "You have come to the only One who can restore your vessel, and so it shall be! Your vessel will be restored!" He seemed to know my thoughts, as he added, "Dear one, I already knew the condition of your vessel before you brought it to Me. I am prepared to restore this vessel, and you will be able to use it for the rest of your life to come!"

I then exclaimed "Master! I have compromised this vessel! I know how I've misused and abused it. I caused most of the damage to it! There are so many cracks that it's totally unusable! But, please help my unbelief! I want to believe!" As tears burned down my face, the Master looked into my eyes and said, "My dear child, that may have played a part, but I see beyond what you or anyone else sees! I see the true worth and value of every vessel! This vessel was made for honor! It shall fulfill its destiny!"

Awestruck, I watched as he laid open His hands and began to work on the vessel. I winced upon seeing his hands; though they were strong, they were also red, blistered, and scarred. He nodded as if He was reading my thoughts again, saying, "My child, these hands have restored many a vessel for the Alpha and Omega. I am not distressed over these hands, for Integrity has been restored to every vessel that has been brought to Me; it is My blood that is the necessary component in the restoration process. Without My blood, there can be no restoration to any vessel! I, and I alone, have the great and Eternal Seal of the Head Master! He blesses me and crowns Me for this work that I do. Therefore, now, my child, I shall restore your vessel. No longer shall you carry shame. This vessel was marked for royalty and honor, so it shall be!"

I watched Him work. His eyes "flashed" as the pottery wheel spun over heat. Sweat and blood minced with the clay of the vessel in His hands. The fire that was underneath caused contaminants to rise up to the surface. He drew out the contaminants with a steady rhythm of His hands. I watched sweat droplets fall from His brow. I knew that He had to be experiencing pain from using His raw hands to reshape and blend the new clay with the old. My heart skipped a beat each time that I noticed His hands passing over certain areas because they reminded me of times when I had put my vessel in harm's way. Also, as His hands smoothed over certain other places, I was reminded of times when others had harmed my vessel. While I was remembering these things, His face turned toward me, and He said, "Dear one, your sins are forgiven. But, know this, those who have harmed you must also be forgiven by you. What I do for you, I want you to do for them." He then told me, "The Deceiver has manipulated and enslaved many a vessel that was called for service to the Alpha and Omega. Today, you are being set free from all the wrongs you've committed, and from all the harm that your vessel has suffered. When this process is complete, go and tell others what I have done for you. Tell them that I am waiting for them, and that I look forward to restoring vessels for them, just as I am doing for you today. Remember Me always."

I confessed all my sins to Him and surrendered. I also prayed for everyone who had ever harmed me. At the close of our meeting, we broke out with songs of praise to the Alpha and Omega! I knew that I had a bond with the Master – one which I had never experienced before! One that would never be broken! All fear and torment that I had felt for so many years was GONE! His perfect love drove out all fear! When the time came for me to leave Him, my vessel was fully restored! How thankful I was! I had peace, and I sensed that He would always be with me – wherever I would go! My vessel was my gift and provision from Him. I had Living Water to share with all who were willing to drink! I knew that I would never run out of this Water – for the more I poured out, the more He filled my vessel back up! It was phenomenal! I was so satisfied, and I loved to point others to the Most Wonderful Restorer – my Master, my Lord and Savior: Jesus Christ!

PRELUDE TO:

It is I, Jesus

Have you ever felt invisible? Invisible to those you cherish and love? Invisible to the world, your community, your family, your church, to God?? To quote a dear friend of mine, "It feels really, really bad!" You may have had the following thoughts: "Am I worthwhile?" "Am I valuable?" "Do I matter?" "Does ANYBODY see me? – REALLY see ME!?" "Does anybody care?"

The bottom line is: There's so much more to you and me than most people realize!!! I find that many people have gone through times in their life when they felt extremely alone and/or deeply disappointed, and it may have seemed there was no one who could truly help them. This essay comes precisely from such a place. Does God see <u>me</u>? Does God hear <u>me</u>? Does God even care?

Life seems to forge ahead with or without us – not missing a beat, and at times even "mowing us down" by unexpected tragedy, stress, or loss. Many times, now, I've heard people say they were so alone: in their marriage, in their family, in their neighborhood, in their jobs, even in their churches! Sometimes there's a place where no other human can go with us or comfort us. Sometimes we sense that people are pulling away from us when we've entered certain private, dark, and difficult places – places where consolation feels out of reach. However, these very places can become the holiest of places! – Places where altars are built and memory stones are laid. Places where <u>we</u> can actually encounter God for ourselves! Places where we can "hear" His voice! Places, that, when we hold nothing back, but instead, get "dirt honest" with God – He actually reveals Himself; He sees us! And, despite all of our baggage, He acknowledges us and loves us anyway! He then takes us deep into the depths of a real and personal love. There, we find His magnificent gifts of grace, peace, acceptance, love, forgiveness, and unimaginable power to become overcomers! Oh, if only we could get a glimpse of ourselves through His eyes, instead of our own . . . We would then hear the words of the following poem:

Part I: It Is I, Jesus

I see you! You think no one sees you!
I hear you! You think no one hears!
I hold you, even when you think no one is near.
I love you, though you think no one truly loves you.
It is I, yes, truly I.
I have stood by . . . patiently.
I have longed, as your own heart has longed, for us to be together!
I yearn and desire for us to be one.
It has burned within you, but you have misunderstood.
You have looked, but misplaced it.
But I know you.
I know you best.
This is why no one else can satisfy the desire you have,
 inexpressible in your heart.

It is I! Yes! You begin to understand.
You discern correctly! Yes, I, Jesus!
I have loved you since you were in your mother's womb,
but you thought that I had forgotten you altogether.
No, I could never forget you.
You are my desire come forth.
You are my beauty. You are my heart!
You are an expression of my love!
And, while I gifted you to love others,
Your devotion belongs to Me.
Receive Me, my love, my dear one.
Do you feel overwhelmed?
I will cause you no harm!
You will only be fully satisfied when you are immersed in My love!
Allow me to pour out my love upon you!
Know, too, that those who surround you will also benefit

from my outpouring. For I love you, my precious.
Yes. You are perceiving it now . . .
I truly love you, my fair one.
See how I cover you with my love . . . You are not naked.
I clothe you with My purity . . . You need not be ashamed.
It is I . . . your true lover!
Let me come to you and fill you up, my love.
Be complete in Me and you will lack no good thing!
I am yours, and you are Mine . . .
Be Mine forever, love . . . my sweet one, my precious!

Forever,

Jesus

Part II: My Response

I thought You didn't see me.
I thought You didn't know.
I felt so forsaken, and had nowhere to go.
I mistook others for you;
I left you, instead of them.
I've reaped the whirlwind over and again.

But in a quiet, desolate place
my enemies released me.
Then, Your soft voice I heard calling,
and the desert felt like home.
I am not alone.
You love me!
My secrets are like billboards – open to the sky.
My desires, no longer hidden. Your spirit does not lie.
You! You are my everything!
You meet all my need!
Here in the place where You alone comfort, love, and lead.

My hope is in no other . . .
no other one will do . . .
my love is truly You, Lord.
My love is truly You.

Part III: Final Meditation

To the Lord:

I see You!
I love You!
I like being in Your Presence;
How beautiful You are, O' Rose of Sharon.
You stand as a glorious warrior in Your Sovereignty;
yet, You are so gentle to love me
and take me as Your own special one.
You cover me in the shadow of Your strength.
In Your great strength,
You don't cease to love passionately or compassionately.

Your mercy endures.
Your Grace is a scepter of light and life to whomever You extend it to.
By it, our nakedness is clothed and our darkness is made light.
Your word is as a bulwark: immovable, solid, and stabilizing.
By it, I endure the torrents of life – with its storms and trials.
Your Grace and Mercy keep me firmly,
especially while assailants assault.

For You, O' Lord, are greater than all my enemies.
Who is like You?
You exceed them all by Your great poise, strength, dignity, and glory.
Praise surrounds You, radiating as gold brilliance.
The fragrance of Mir and spices bathe You;
therefore, my senses are utterly intoxicated.
My strength fails, and my heart would stop
if it were not for You upholding me.
My breath would cease, yet You sustain me,
I am satisfied with Your food.

(Thy Word, O' Lord, is my food: the Bread of Heaven,
and I am satisfied. It gives me life.)
You, indeed, make me have hind feet upon the highest heights.
I flee from my enemies on Your Holy Mountain.
The crack and crag are my footing.
I do not fall because You preserve me.
I am Yours.
You love me with tender mercies.
I am overwhelmed!
Never let me go from Your Presence, O' Lord!
Let me look upon You and Your love, always.
You are my all in all.
In You I hope for the day.
In the night, I may find trouble or anxiety . . .
but I search for You . . .
You let me find You, while You hold me in the hollow of Your hand;
here, I find safety, rest and peace.
Let me never depart from You.
I will rejoice in You and Your love!
I will proclaim Your beauty and righteousness to all generations!
I will praise You! You are kind!
I will tell of Your great deeds!
Oh how my heart flourishes in Your love!
You revive me from death.
Whom do I have in heaven besides You?
And on all the earth there is none I desire but You!

I am love-sick;
let me never go without Your love!
Sustain me with Your kisses!
Hold me and let me be Yours always and forever!
For I love You, my Master and Lord.

Yes, I am Yours, and You are mine.
I praise You with all my breath!
And I thank you forever!
Hallelujah!

Mourning "The Child"

I see her in my mind's eye like it was yesterday:
always, she is curious and open to people – without prejudice.
She is innocent, sincere and warm.
And she's been missing now for far too many years.

This morning I awoke from a dream:
I found her: She was talking to a stranger.
A man I'd never seen before.
I was running after her, trying to stop her. I worried she was in danger.
"Don't talk to strangers, remember?!" I yelled.
But when I caught up, I saw only the Stranger.
He wasn't anything I thought he was.
And . . . she, she was gone.
For some reason, I forgot about the little girl.
I found myself, in the next moment, sitting crossed-legged on the floor
in the presence of the Stranger.
And He intrigued me. He captivated me.
He spoke with great wisdom, and exuded grace and patience,
of such I'd never encountered before.
All the while,
He was very in-tune with all that was going on around Him.
He spoke of things that truly mattered.
I didn't want to leave Him now.
I didn't want the conversation to end.
I watched and I listened.
He not only interacted with me, but with everyone
near him or going by, as if He knew each one so well.
He understood people from every walk of life,
exampled by what I saw.
Amazingly enough, He knew and understood me!

Despite all the idiosyncrasies and flaws we, as people, have,
there was no hesitation in His interactions.
He risked His heart and love,
without regret whether He was rejected or not.

In sitting there with Him, and watching so many people come and go,
I observed:
- They spoke familiarly with him like old friends.
- There were so many differences in their ages and personalities.
- Everyone was comfortable and happy around Him.

It was obvious that He was well liked and respected.
If I described His physical attributes, his style of clothing, you'd
understand why I was alarmed when I first saw the little girl
going toward Him. For, while He wore a button-down, collared shirt,
and khaki pants, neither appeared to have seen a washing machine
for quite some time; His clothing seemed dingy.
There were no shoes on His feet.
He hadn't shaved his face in a while, either. Regardless of this first
impression, He drew you right in immediately with the way in which
He spoke, as if He saw through your soul and knew you deeply.
He knew what to say and what you needed to hear.
He was genuinely interested in your life; at the same time,
He was so matter of fact about it.
He was that approachable. That friendly. And He genuinely cared.
Again . . . I didn't want the conversation to end.
But in this dream, I had to leave.
I was hearing my children call for me.
I remember trying to get His "number" so I could call upon Him later.
Then my body was whisked away and I awoke from the dream.
The clock by my bed read 4:50 a.m.
I had 40 more minutes before I actually had to get out of bed!
I prayed. I asked Jesus to meet with me today.
(I had much of the day to myself for a change.)

I closed my eyes, and fell back to sleep.
My alarm went off. I walked upstairs to the kitchen,
started coffee, bacon, and eggs. I stopped:
I remembered the girl, who's been missing all these years!
And then two vivid memories came to me from long ago [true story]:

The first one: A lovely lady came by the local park.
The "little girl" had been sitting alone, but near enough to see her. This
lady was collecting wild flowers and tying them together in long
strands. Intrigued, the little girl drew near, asking if she could do this,
too. And together they made necklaces, bracelets, and wreaths to
crown their heads. I can't remember any conversation.

The second vivid memory came to me behind the other:
At that same park, a Chinese man came. Again, this "little girl" was
curious. She smiled and greeted him. He sat down next to her. Sitting
cross-legged in the grass they made small talk. He was very nice.
Smiling. Sharing where he was from. She was enchanted, and he
didn't mind answering her many, many, questions.

In an instant, as the memories replayed in my head, I exclaimed:
"Jesus! I wonder if these were angels then, "entertaining me unaware!"
That which is spoken of in the scriptures!

What happened to that "little girl?!"
Tears were spilling from my eyes. I could not contain them.
How did I become this hard, indifferent, distrustful, and CYNICAL
person today? I looked in the mirror, and the little girl dimmed in my
memory. She was almost a stranger to me now.
Was that really me?
I vaguely remember.
Yet I do remember: How I was always so "smiley" on the outside,
while insecure on the inside. I remember, too, how people I
encountered could be so different from one another,

and yet similar at the same time.
Different in their appearances, styles, accents, and cultures,
and yet the same when it came to friendship
and emotions of fear, love, regret, and pride.
I knew back then that God made us.
I knew He really cared about people.
I also knew there was something to learn from everyone I met.
I knew we were all made in the image and likeness of God.

But, as I look at myself now, I've seen in more recent years, how I've searched for a way out, or the slightest reason that I should not trust others. I did not want to take any more chances or risks because of all the hurts I'd sustained over the years! I now looked for any clue that justified me excusing myself from bothering to know someone at all.
I'd lost faith in people . . .
I'd simply lost faith.
Now in recent weeks, I have been very bothered.
I am very bothered because – after reading the Beatitudes again . . .
Jesus gets to my core with that one verse He must know "gets to me."
It is: "Blessed are the pure in heart, for they shall see God."
He taps into a desire I cling to from childhood.
A desire to be pure and clean,
so, ultimately, I may see the God I love and want, the God who has loved me. He for whom I long for more than anything ever!! I have to love whom He loves. I must have a pure heart.

I feel like innocence is lost; the "little girl" is lost!
Can she ever be recovered?!
Can I ever see God?
I weep bitterly.
I groan in anguish.
"Jesus!" I cry. And again, "Jesus!!!"
Come meet with me today, Jesus!
Help me hear, help me see – again!

Let me be that little girl in my heart – again!
The one that trusted You and believed the good in people.
Jesus said to me "You are clean because of the words I've spoken to you. Enter the Kingdom as a little child."
I want to lose the "cynical adult" and give place back to the child who trusts her heavenly Father. The child who sees the value of those created in the image of God, respecting each one.
Seeing the gift of each and every person I meet in this life.

So here's my heart, Lord. Heal it, fill it, use it for Your purposes.
Let me see others through Your eyes, and as Your little child again.
Amen.

Forbid Them Not

As He scooped them up in His arms,
He gave their dreams wings to fly:
"Forbid them not to come," He said,
"for in me they'll never die."

For of such is the kingdom of God.
For of such is the kingdom of God.

A little girl runs from her broken home.
She runs and cries and seems alone.
Jesus will come, little one, pray.
Jesus will come, heal, and make a way.

For of such is the kingdom of God.
For of such is the kingdom of God.

A little boy lost inside a man.
Jesus came, stretching out His hand.
The little boy grasped it, asked Him to stay.
And Jesus healed the man that day.

Children everywhere are lost at what to do.
They seek to find answers: real and true.
Jesus says "Behold, I make all things new.
I am here for you, I am here for you."

For of such is the kingdom of God.
For of such is the kingdom of God.

Intellectuals and doubters struggle to believe
in a God that's so personal, whom they think they don't need.

"The sick need a doctor," said Jesus. "See, you are broken, too!
That's why I had to come. To heal and make you new.
Only enter as a child, trusting and mild.
For of such is the kingdom of God!"
["But Jesus said, Suffer little children, and forbid them not, to come
unto me: for of such is the kingdom of heaven. Matthew 19:14"]

between two little girls
(In honor and with love, for my dear mom)

Angelina, little girl,
golden blond with kinky curl.
Momma was a teacher,
met a dream gone wrong.
Daddy was a boiler maker,
tough and strong.
Momma left her Texas home
for South Carolina, where you were born.

Amongst strangers and hidden from play,
you had to grow up before your day.
Angelina, reach out to me;
I will be your friend.
Angelina, come out of the shadows;
God will bring your sorrows to an end.
Angelina, it's hard to trust, I know . . .
But there's a place both safe and sound
where we two can go.

Standing in the shadows
little raga-muffin doll,
eyes filled with tears and knowledge,
which robbed your little girl smile.
Protecting your brothers, and little sisters, too,
living in the "thorny" bush, Life was not good to you.
Your eyes beheld violence: all in black and blue;
storm clouds never ceasing but hovering over you.

Then womanhood overtook you.
You found someone to marry –
unknowing your past abuse –

you were left to carry.
He didn't know or understand
your pain and childhood years –
a happy-go-lucky man.
Hiding his own childhood fears,
a brew so unsuspecting,
as years buried little Angelina girl,
lovely blue eyes, blond and kinky curl.

I came to know you, Angelina.
I saw you through the Father's eyes.
He told me that He wept over you,
and longed to right the lies.
It was never His desire for a little girl to see
or experience such nightmares,
which even terrify me.
Angelina, I know the little girl within you –
crouching in a corner, hiding inside your heart.
I want to be your friend and draw you out again!
Reach out to me!
I will be your friend!
Come out of the shadows,
let the light come in!
God will bring your sorrows to an end.
It's hard to trust, I know,
but there's a place both safe and sound
where we two can go.
See up on that hill so fair?
The Shepherd Jesus bids us there.
The Balm of Gilead is in His hand.
It will heal and comfort as we enter in.

Be my friend, Angelina, enter in.
Angelina takes the balm.
The Shepherd embraces her . . .
embraces my mom.
Now we enter in, not as mother and daughter . . .
but as a forever friendship, between two little girls.

Rebecca

PRELUDE

On June 6th, 2001, I lost a very close friend, Loretta Lynn. At the age of 33, she died of a sudden heart attack that no one expected! Four young children were left without their mommy. Megan was only about 12 years old, Jon was about 11, while Rebecca was only 5, and Jacob was 3. It was heart wrenching to see her husband and kids go through this ordeal of living without her for years to come. I, like many other friends of hers, reached out and helped in every way possible. My family and Loretta's family had remained close over the years. I wrote the following poem for Rebecca – aware of such a tender age to experience so great a loss, and far too young to handle it. I gave it to her later on. It was like a prayer. I wrote the oldest two children, and reached out to them around the same time.

As time passed, I spoke to all of them, often, about what their mom was like: her creativity, her laughter, and her desires for them, which she shared with me and wrote about in her journals. Little Rebecca, whom everyone called "Becca," was a "sing-songy" little girl! She loved to dress up in princess dresses, with accessories, and heels . . . as she danced around the house singing. Her mom got a huge delight out of this, taking photo "ops" as often as possible! It has been 14 long years now. Megan is married and has a delightful son named Shane. Jon is in the National Guard and was recently married. Rebecca is finishing college and works so hard; she has even bought her own car. Jacob will finish High School this year, and works as a lifeguard over the summer. Larry has struggled so hard over the years, but he keeps fellowship with friends and church family; I believe he's found love again. Loretta would be pleased, I think, to see how her family is doing now.

Recently I remembered Loretta's birthday. She would have been 48. I miss my friend. This poem is in honor of her life. She was a godly woman! She prayed fervently for her family and children. She posted scriptures around her house that stated her prayerful desires. I look forward to the time when her family and I get to see her again! She often chided me to publish my writings. Well, here you go, my dear friend. I miss you!

Rebecca

I sit and hold you in my arms
as tears stream down my face.
I hug you tightly and you respond
with such a glad and warm embrace.

Such "little frame"
to hold such pain.
Such a fragile, tender soul.
While I, with all my hope and might,
try to be a momma's hug for now.

It's only been a few short months
since your momma's unexpected death.
We grasp at the knowledge: "She's in heaven,"
while we each choke upon our breath.

What will life now hold for you,
O' fragile and tender soul?
I believe her seeds of prayer and toil
will take root and fill this hole.

I know the Jesus your momma knew.
If this one thing I could impart to you:
In Him you can live, hope, and believe;
He promised never to forsake you or leave.

Little angel girl with melodious gift of song,
I will never cease in prayer and love,
though this shadowed path seems long.
Hold tight, sweet child of heaven.
Cry as often as you must.

Portraits of Hope!

Cry a river if its forces clear
obstacles unjust.

Before you lay a blessed way,
which only you can trod,
it is a most rewarding place: along Almighty God.

I love you. I treasure you . . .
my best friend's little girl.
And I trust this God we love and serve
to see you through this world.

God's Man
(For Larry)

PRELUDE

Larry is a friend to me and my family; he was the husband of my dear and close friend, Loretta. We celebrated their 10th wedding anniversary together as they renewed their vows. Tragically, Loretta passed away suddenly in September of 2001. Our families shared a lot of memories together before and after this tragedy.

Before this tragedy, Loretta and I prayed for our families daily, and we encouraged one another. We shared our feelings. We were "kindred spirits," and had so much in common with one another. The poem that follows was written in 1997, when Larry was going through a tough transition. Loretta wanted me to pray for Larry at the time. I wanted to encourage him as my brother in Christ, and so wrote the following poem for him. (Before she passed, Loretta had expressed to me how she wanted him to know his value and worth both as a dad and a husband, including how important, though difficult, both these roles were!) Larry has kept this writing. I saw it in his home while visiting him some time ago. I was blessed to see he had held onto it!

We all need to be encouraged that God has a plan for each of us, and if He has made a plan, He will also make the necessary provisions for the plan to be fulfilled! Take heart, dear one, take heart! He will see you through!

God's Man

You were chosen.
You are God's man.
You will overcome
by the blood of the Lamb.
You have all you'll need:
a grace sufficient, indeed.
You will fight and you will stand.
For you, my brother, are God's man!

His provisions meet your innermost desire.
You were born of water and baptized by fire.
You are to your wife
a messenger of life,
and when you are yielded with loving hand,
you will succeed! You are God's man!

You are the archer of your offspring.
You are to them a messenger from the King.
As you aim them, far they'll sail.
Through great heights, God's word will prevail!
So, know your worth, walk out the plan.
You are chosen, you are God's man!

HANDS

Her hands were strong, not shy of work,
faithful and gentle, while not always soft.
Love filled these hands that raised me up –
hands unlike any others . . .
these hands are my Mother's.

His hands were visibly strong . . .
hands of a working man –
callous and rough,
smelling of oil or ink in his labor.
Bigger hands than mine, so strong to catch me or hold me up,
I felt safe in these hands.
I wasn't sad . . .
these hands belonged to my Dad.

On the day he took my hands into his,
a band of love encircled my finger.
A promise began.
Hands that understand –
not perfect, as anyone could see,
but these hands are my husband's, always loving me.

6 little hands reach out to me –
trusting me to guide and lead.
Dependent little hands, that grow and grow.
How in the world could they possibly know . . .
the depth and lengths to which I'd go
to protect these little hands from trouble.
These tender little hands, I'll rescue on the double!
I love them all the while they're here . . .
these hands of my children . . . so very dear.

These hands, the first to form me.
And though they are mentioned last . . .
they are a lifetime and forever,
and keep me in caring grasp. –
Hands of my Savior,
faithful and true . . .
without these hands,
what could I do?
They created my breath and bore my sorrows . . .
nail pierced and scarred . . .
they assure my tomorrows.
Thank You, Lord
for all of these hands . . .
destined from above . . .
hands that tell the best of stories . . .
hands engraved with Your great love!

Jacqueline Marie Sparaco

Consider Winter

I used to equate Winter with indifference.
For it is most void of feeling, even color.
Besides being cold and lifeless,
I find it too lengthy!
(It is equal in length to the other seasons, I know,
but far too long for me!)

Winter leaves its mark with frozen lakes, silent woods,
and leafless trees.
Activity ceases in its chill!
Winter winds whistle and howl, echoing Winter's dreary song,
and whether Valley or Mountain Peak, it shows favor to none!
The Atmosphere's once energetic charge wanes in Winter.
Winter certainly seems the most unproductive of all the seasons!
It only hides earth and stream in snow and ice.
And the days! How short are the days of Winter!
Driving us indoors too soon, while enabling the night to steal our light!

These traits of Winter sadden me.
I ache for Spring!
I savor Summer!
I delight in Fall!
But Winter? I believe it robs me of joy!

Yes, I said to myself:
"Winter is a thief of light, warmth, and nature's beauty!
Always it chases me inside with its frigid ways!"
Winter seems to have nothing good to offer, I was convinced.
All I saw in Winter was: void and emptiness.

On a day, when I quieted my soul,
I was thoughtful of the Master of Seasons.
I inquired of Winter's purpose!
In soft whispers, I heard the Spirit say to me;
upon hearing, I gave consideration.
"Winter gives more grace!" said the Spirit.
"For Winter gives rest.
It nurtures regeneration.
Although activity slows above ground,
in its dormant months there IS growth and activity:
BENEATH the surface!
In quietness Winter does its good work.
Not boastful, Winter often eludes the gaze and praise of man.
But Winter has an important part to play.
Because Winter facilitates life in the unseen.
Winter works WITII nature, while slowing it down.
Winter teaches us patience, too –
often working unseen upon the surface and beneath!
Winter knows its part is important.
Not only giving rest and necessary pause . . .
winter forgives – erasing blemishes and imperfections,
changing even landscape and its dominance.
Winter relinquishes some work,
to begin a fresh new work for the future.
Winter prepares a fresh palette and a new canvas."

A "do over," as I like to call it!

"Winter is an equalizer, pausing growth and production of
"wheat and weed" alike. Winter inspires consideration,
 and again: new beginnings and change.
How often Winter covers the muddied earth, or the poorest,
dirtiest city with the fresh, glistening snow –
making beauty out of every place.

No sunrise is more lovely or brighter than Winter's!
No midnight sky is more blue and velvety, or as gorgeous a display
of diamond-like stars, than Winter's!

Winter's boundaries are meant for good.
Not to rob or steal from the bounty of any other season,
but, rather, to nurture rest and rejuvenation,
leading to fullness and abundance!"

I was wrong about you, Winter! I see you with new eyes!
I will wait upon your good deeds and appreciate your role
in the cycle of seasons!

I have this thought, too, in addressing the "Winter" that comes in the
lateness of our lives:
Do not despise Winter . . .
It's labor and fruits may seem modest, even bare . . .
but when Winter completes its cycle of work,
rest assured, glory follows unlike any time before!

Bodies may slow, strength may weaken,
shadows increase, eyes grow dim,
our surface no longer shows the youthfulness we feel within:
Patience! For after our failing outward shell, comes a greater one!
After Winter comes Spring . . .
and a New life begins.
And after the Winter of our lives, Spring will be forever!
Winter "seasons" the seasons . . . well!

Hidden

Look at me.
Really look at me.
Don't just pass me by.
I don't want your pity,
token well wishes,
or sad-gestured sigh.
Don't walk by me in disregard.
Don't toss me in the "pile."
There's so much more to me
than the twisted body,
crooked, drooling smile.
I absorb the world around me.
I listen to your words, too.
I have something to offer,
there's still plenty I can do.
So take the time to know me.
Stretch your hands over the wall.
I may be simple to the naked eye.
I may be profound, after all.

"Mary"
(Prelude)

Mary is a friend I met while attending a private school of art. She had been painting for many years by this time. Her style and excellence were so evident in her paintings! We first met at one of our Art shows because we didn't attend class the same days. Not long after, maybe a year or two later, Mary needed a ride to class and I lived close by, so we went together. I felt a strange familiarity with her until I realized what it was! Upon hearing her last name, it dawned on me that sometime in 1995, 7 or 8 years before meeting her, I had met someone who had told me about her. She liked my drawing skills and wanted me to meet this seasoned artist! Unfortunately I was really insecure about picking up the phone to call Mary then! Now here I was driving Mary to our class! When we put two and two together . . . this lady, Jane, was Mary's neighbor, and they had stayed in touch even though Jane had moved away! On our drives to art class, Mary began to share her life stories with me. Raising her six children. Experiencing the loss of a child, 9 months in the womb, stillborn. I also learned Mary had had a very difficult childhood and life. These were clearly her better years, and yet, over these years, her health was becoming more and more challenging. When I wrote the following "Tribute" to Mary, I thought I was about to lose her! She had been diagnosed with lung cancer, and it had spread throughout her body! I took her to her chemotherapies and doctor appointments. In my tribute, I had to say what I needed to say before it was too late! Mary was rushed to the Emergency Room many times from 2010 through early 2014. In this tribute, I wanted Mary to see her worth and value! I shared it with her children first to get their feedback. I explained to Mary, that, at the time, I thought I was losing her and I wanted to write something to show what she meant to me and others! She smiled, and with a gleam in her eye said, "That's OK, honey!" "Thank you!" My dear friend, Mary passed away February 26th, 2015. I feel privileged to have been able to be by her side to the end. Her family has been so kind to me and inclusive of me in her "Celebration of Life." Ms. Mary was a good friend to me and a great comfort after losing my own parents in 2010 and 2011. So this is my tribute to a lady who now is 83 years old!

A TRIBUTE TO MARY:

Did I tell you?
You've inspired me! Artist to artist!
Did I tell you?
You mean so much to me and you are important in my life!
Did I tell you? I admire you for the woman, mother, and artist you are!
Did I tell you? Your life has just amazed me!
You shared your story with me, Mary.
I've gleaned and pondered so much from you!
You have survived great turmoil and troubles.
Yes, I am amazed as I ponder the road you've travelled to HERE.
Sadly, I see the light of life relinquishing its crisp energy and power,
as evening shadows fall upon us, blanketing us with the night.
I feel you slipping . . . away – away from my grasp, Mary!
How long do I have to savor our time together?
For I seem to now lose you a little each day.
I don't know what to do with this reality.
I find I am perplexed.
My heart begs to refuse it.
Still more questions swirl in my thoughts.
Have I said all that I wanted to say?
Do you know how much you are loved?
Do you know your value and worth?
At the end of life, idiosyncrasies or failings fade to mist;
yet all the seemingly "nothings" and small things . . .
become so much more: "somethings" and special.
The everyday "ordinary" and simple find their way
into my heart as "thankful moments," precious memories being made.
In these moments where we laugh, or cry, or sit side by side quietly:
together, we linger here.
We celebrate and embrace each and every one.
These are the things that matter to us:

family, friends, love, and laughter.
These are the "meaningful," held dear in our hearts.
Not so fleeting as money, success, or fame.
Rather, it is what is lasting, that even upon our death beds, we keep:
it is who we loved, how we loved, and where love abides.
I don't want to say goodbye . . .
I want to say, until we meet again,
in a better place,
at a better time.
We all leave a legacy.
Mary, do you know yours?
I am aware of your legacy.
I've learned some of it from your children and your sisters.
I've seen it displayed in your lovely, girlish,
and day-dreamy paintings.
So vibrant, so brilliant, are the walls of your dwelling.
Your home encapsulates your life:
those four walls of your home are the Canvas of your Life,
exuding your finest work!
From the surrounding photographs of the ones you love,
to all the subjects you have painted and portrayed.
Every time I enter this dwelling, it feels like sanctuary!
You are an artist, Mary!! In every way!
Your life and love are on exhibit.
They reveal your appreciation for all that's beautiful and fine!
All this emphasized by brush and stroke!
No, you will not be forgotten!
Your life, on this side of heaven,
forged from a very difficult past,
is likened to a masterful embroidery,
here visible only from behind:
purpose can appear distorted by the twists, turns,
and knots of threading;
however, made clear, by and by,

showing in its finality absolute magnificence!
Especially at the "Great Reveal" when we meet again in Heaven!
This side of heaven isn't always clear, but, by and by, we will see!
I love you, my friend, my fellow artist!
I have learned and gleaned so much from you.
Thank you for sharing your life with me!

Love,
Jackie Sparaco

A Miracle for John
(Prelude)

I wrote this song for a dear friend of mine. He experienced many trials as a young boy. He was born albino, legally blind, and was diagnosed with diabetes in his youth. He was the target of bad jokes and cold shoulders while growing up. I met John when I was 19 years old. It was shortly after I believed in Jesus Christ. John was a Christian, too. He wrote his own songs: lyrics and music. John was not only talented artistically, but very intelligent for his years. We volunteered at nursing homes – leading worship on Sundays. We spent time sharing ideas and writings. After a few years, John had the opportunity to go to Liberty University. Family and friends alike were excited for him. Unfortunately, another tragedy befell John. While returning home for a Thanksgiving Holiday, John and his friend, who was driving, crashed into an eighteen wheeler during a bad fog on a Virginia Highway. John had a broken neck, broken thigh, and other breaks and fractures. I drove with a friend to Virginia to see him at the hospital. John was hooked up to so many tubes, wires, and devices, along with a ventilator. Upon seeing him, I immediately felt dizzy and almost hit the floor. I gathered myself together and prayed over him. By December, doctors predicted that John would be in a vegetated state if and when he came out of the coma he was in. I spent many a late hour crying and praying for John. His parents were drained. I felt drained. I remember opening my Bible and praying for him. I came upon a verse that seemed to jump off the pages at me! It was Psalm 118: 16 and 17. It said, "The LORD's right hand is lifted high; the LORD's right hand has done mighty things! I will not die but live, and will proclaim what the LORD has done." It resonated through me strongly. I called his mom in joy and tears, sharing this verse. We held hope that John was going to recover. I then wrote the following song, "A Miracle for John." Another friend played guitar to it, and we recorded it. It was my prayer. We took the recording to his parents and they played it at the hospital.

This song-prayer was answered! John came out of his coma! John began to write his communications. After intense and long therapies, he began talking, walking, and doing more than the doctors ever expected. This isn't the end of John's story. John had also experienced a brain injury, which triggered depression. Therefore, he had to work on overcoming depression and grieving some losses, such as not returning to school, and not getting around as well as he once had. I am thankful for the answered prayer that John did "not die but live."

A Miracle For John (Answered Prayer!)

Lord, I come before your Holy throne,
placing hope in You and You alone.
Raising up a prayer and longing, too,
that this overwhelming trial
will be heard and healed by You!

We need a miracle for John,
a miracle for John.
He's only just begun to live.
And as that miracle for John
begins to manifest . . .
all glory and honor to You!

Lord, You know the kind of life he's had, and
how much he's longed to live to make you glad.
His struggles and his cries
are now pouring out my eyes.
I turn to You in trust, and plead:
we need a miracle for John,
a miracle for John.
He's only just begun to live.
And as that miracle for John
begins to manifest . . .
all glory and honor to You!

Lord, increase my faith and help me see
Your miracles didn't end at Calvary.
The life our Jesus gave
is the very life that saves
and heals a broken heart,
and sets a captive free.

We need a miracle for John,
 a miracle for John.
We know that You can raise him up
and, with that miracle for John,
thanks and praise we'll bring!
Many more may come!
Many more may sing!
"Thanks for the miracle for John!"

A Rose

Fragrant and lovely,
gentle yet strong.
Like a rose, you are pleasing
and worthy of song!
As delicate as the petals, reflecting God's grace,
you free up a smile to a solemn face.

You are a sister, a mom,
a well-seasoned blend
of mercy and love . . .
a welcoming friend!

All that I see, when I savor your presence,
is a generous vessel bearing Jesus's essence!

It hurts to say goodbye
when miles try to part!
But there really is no distance –
when we're so close in heart.
We have this confidence, each one knows,
in the mystery of life, God's wisdom brings repose.
And you, dear lady, are as lovely as a rose!

I know He is cultivating, making us His own.
Such a wonderful Gardener, we are never alone!
Nurturing and increasing us, as He pulls out the weeds,
filling us to overflowing, so we'll sow more seeds.

My favorite of flowers, which I most enjoy,
(Surely the Lord does too),
are the Roses of His likeness . . . bursting with fragrance,
and one I've found, in the color of YOU!

I love you, my friend . . . precious rose true!
Know I'll always cherish my memories of YOU!

Love,
in Jesus,
The True Rose of Sharon.

A god called 'me'

My thoughts race downward, descending.
My heart feels vacant
and my energy's spent.
A merciless incumbent
with a false beat of truth
has me swirling and twirling –
keeps sweet peace aloof!
 I, by my own insistence,
live a doctrine of self –
escaping true knowledge
and its bountiful wealth.
All my energy, in its ebb and flow,
sinks deep in self-seeking –
missing knowledge for woe.
For man cannot,
nor ever that be,
a god to himself,
nor a god to me!

For I, in my toil, have hastily wrought,
forgetting what Christ, my Savior,
purchased and bought.
This Eternal Godhead: Father, Spirit, Son –
together, these three are Holy, in One.
Share the Story of Life,
which for me should be:
God exalted, and death to "me!"
The Lord is love, eternal in His worth;
He gives life after death, and hope in new birth.
Take me now,
Savior dear,

to waiting altar.
I will not fear
that I die, forgo my own desire,
and lose all sin-heap in Your cleansing fire.
What say you, Oh man?
Do you not see?
The folly and fodder in a god called "me?"
Nothing of life will accompany you there –
in wasted hours of selfish care.
Do not dawdle or linger
in the self's false light:
you will only go deeper
into cold empty night.
Raise up a cry from your anguished soul,
and humble thy self-claimed fame!
There is but one Maker, by whom you are called!
In Him there's beauty, when we bear His name!

Take hold of the altar,
Lie down upon there!
Don't doubt, don't falter,
but release all care!

He comes quickly
to redeem your tattered soul!
In ashes after fire,
what will He see?
No wicked, no more;
no god of "me!"
Save beauty for ashes.
Save gold for stone.
Save the one He loves purely;
save Him alone.
Goodbye to the god of "me!" Lord, let it be!

He Loved Me All Along
(Prelude)

If you enjoy the Psalms, as I do, you find great comfort in them. Before the comfort, though, you might relate first to the heart-cries of the Psalmist due to troubles, anxiety, sorrow, or even the despair you sometimes face. When I wrote "He Loved Me All Along," it was upon reflection of such Psalms that I gained a wonderful truth! You may notice many a Psalm begins with cries of injustice, pain, conflict, or turmoil. Then you find that they recall and remember all God has done, from past to present. It is in this "remembering" that we realize God is greater than any circumstance!!! Unfortunately, He "shrinks" when our circumstances are magnified! If we reflect, we will see He's been there all along, helping us. We find strength and learn we can trust Him for the rest of our lives. He is greater than all our troubles and struggles. Our hearts find refuge in Him! Take time to recall and remember all the prayers answered, and all the promises He's given through His Word, such as: He will "never leave nor forsake you. [Hebrews 13:5]" For, truly, truly, my friend, He has loved us all along!

He Loved Me All Along

Through pain-filled days and foggy haze,
You were loving me.
During lonely trials and rocky miles,
You were loving me.
Threats didn't come to pass and sorrows didn't last
because You were loving me.
I acted the fool, trying to be "cool,"
but You still loved me.

A friend saw me, knowing I needed You.
He told me You were true.
I learned You were for real;
with my heart I could finally feel
that You were loving me.

Sad to say, I drifted away.
I placed all others ahead of You.
Then my depression grew,
but You still loved me.

So I came to find, as You cleared my mind,
it was You all along,
loving me.
I know You for myself – You're no longer just in a Bible on a shelf.
I began loving You.

Back in the beginning, there was a plan – to set me free.
All along You were loving me!
Now, the hope I carry, while You tarry,
brings me joy and great revelation:
Your kindness and generosity are faithful and true!

From now on – I'll be loving You!
So I'm wanting all which You desire;
You caused this fire!
You brought me up higher!
It's in my heart and in my life: very, very strong;
it was You!
It was You
who loved me all along!!
You're my happy song!
"You love me! You love me!"
Thank You for loving me all along!!

Have you gazed?

Have you gazed into Jesus's eyes today? Have you gazed long enough? When you were driving down the road, and someone cut you off, did you forgive and pray? What did you do? If you cursed or complained, you haven't gazed long enough. While you were working, did you work as unto the Lord? Did you give your best? Or, were you slacking or complaining? If the latter, you haven't gazed long enough. When someone inconvenienced you, and needed your help today, what did you do? Did you take pause from your busy day, helping them on their way? Or did you excuse yourself and just walk away. If the latter, you didn't gaze long enough.

For when you take the time to gaze
into the Lord Jesus's eyes,
you see His LOVE.
You see His FORGIVENESS,
you see His MERCY, ACCEPTANCE, and PATIENCE.
You remember: He sacrificed Himself for you as His scarred pierced hands
reach out to you in your mind's eye.
When you gaze long enough,
you want to do for others what He's done for you:
for you will LOVE,
you will FORGIVE,
You will show MERCY, ACCEPTANCE, and PATIENCE.
When you see the value of others through Christ's eyes,
you will SACRIFICE for them.
And they will benefit, too, from gazing into His eyes!
Don't miss gazing into His eyes today!

Words . . .

Words are very important to me.
For words:
open doors,
pave paths,
build bridges,
and secure a footing from your heart to others.

Words:
They encourage dreams and bring them to fruition.
They are used to recruit ideas –
giving breath, life, and power to them.
Words sow, grow, and may prosper.

The Right Words:
Can regain and win trust.
Can raise optimism.
Can nurture hope.

Words:
They can make a way of escape from oppression.
They can soothe a weary traveler, and calm a troubled soul.

Words are very powerful!
They wield life or death,
they Redeem or condemn.
They can bid hope or despair,
peace or war.
They can shelter or assault,
make a friend or foe.

They can solicit favor or malice,
blessing or curse,
praise or admonishment.

God, fill me with words that produce
an abundance of life to the hearer!
Grant my words to offer sustaining truth and grace to every ear,
while directing all the praise and glory toward You!

Praise is Streaming!!

My cup runs over with the wine of gladness!
Jesus overcame my fears!
He brought me up from the deepest pit!
My God restores my heart and spirit with His strength!
He returns health to my bones.
How good and holy is my God!

Who is worthy to come before you, Most High?
Rejoice, my soul!! Jesus made the way for you!
The Lamb has been sacrificed for all your iniquities!

Oh, God! Now I am acceptable in your sight!
Turn me not away when I cry out to you!
You have saved me, O Lord!
I was in utter confusion and downtrodden in heart.
You shined Your light upon my path.
I had to see things as they truly are!
I was filthy; You made me clean.
Now I am a new creation!
I serve You gladly, O God!
I sing praises!! Hallelujah! Thanks be to You, my Savior and my God!

Final Harbor

Though my face is streaked from tears,
and my eyes stare distant and afar,
take note: it is only for a time.

Though my home sits empty,
silently mourning the loss of busy laughter,
when conversation once filled her walls,
take note: it is only for a time.

I know that a seed must die before it brings forth life.
I know the night is followed by day.
Yet, for this moment, I weep.
And it is only for a time.

With the best of my knowledge I can say:
The course of my life has been charted for me –
long before I ever left my harbor.
I am looking to the One – All-seeing and All-knowing;
"yes" to Him for the journey home.

Some people visit many harbors in a lifetime –
even finding the treasure of true love . . . at least once.
I mourn in this moment for the loss of my treasure!
However, I know my course is mapped;
it is right and good to yield to the Captain and Navigator of my life.
So, I hold this sorrow in these weather beaten hands,
only for a time; yet my sorrow won't last forever.
It will be as a fleeting sparrow when the dawn approaches.
One day, I will recover my treasure, and have greater gain –
at my final Harbor.

"Weeping may endure for a night,
but joy comes in the morning. [Psalm 30:5]"
I will trust the Lord. He is the lover of my heart.

The Answer

I don't have to look in the mirror
to see that I've been crying.
I don't have to read newspapers
to know many are daily dying.
I don't seek to prosper
from the things that don't last.
I don't really wonder that which the world fails to grasp.

It is in the midst of trouble, pain, and fear
that the peace of Jesus is offered us here.

While so much around me crumbles without,
there is a joy I have within:
Coming from Christ my Savior,
I was made free from sin.

It is He who makes one clean before God –
It is Jesus! He once walked this earthly sod.
No greater than He, no greater a love;
may no one despise this Answer from above.

God is the Strength of My Heart

From my heart many voices arise:
some to love,
some to hate.
But within my heart are these two choices:
eternity's doors, or hell's broad gate.
With a balance to weigh, it's this I pray:
to overcome the voice of hate.

In my heart, I'd be a fool
if I didn't allow God's peace to rule.
His peace guards my heart secure.
So, to my Jesus, I implore
as I send supplications, thanksgiving, and praise –
this is my food, both night and day.

And when my heart condemns me more,
God is greater, He will restore.
For my flesh and my heart, they surely fail,
but God is my strength and my portion now.

'Til We Meet Again

(to a daughter whose mother passed away)

O' precious daughter –
daughter, dear.
Don't fret, my darling –
I'll be near.
The page has turned,
a chapter ends;
but the story's not over –
we'll always be friends.
I'm whole and complete.
On this other side,
we'll see one another.
So, don't run or hide.
Your loved ones need you.
I know that they care.
It may appear
that this is unfair.
But, again, stand fast,
for the days are fleeting.
Soon again we'll be together –
'twill be like our first meeting.
These years on the earth –
they cannot compare
to eternity, so awesome
with Our Lord up there.

Hold fast, dear daughter, I've not left for good.
I know you're in shock
and you haven't understood . . .

Portraits of Hope!

There will come a day
all this grief and pain
will be dulled and forgotten
in Jesus's name!

So, for now, my beloved,
go ahead and cry . . .
but just for a little while.
Hug everyone for me,
remember my smile.
Be my shining example of a trusting child.
Your Father in heaven is tender and mild,
He's watching over you and taking care of me.
So, there's no need to fear –
one day you will see!

For Holly

I see you as beautiful!
From your eyes of almond – reflecting Christ's love,
to your smile reflecting a child attentive to His voice,
I see God taking pleasure in you.
I see what a wonder you are.
In the future and in the now – you have a special place –
a special calling that is only yours.
You are set apart.
Be true to God and yourself
'lest you rob us of your beauty.
Don't take on another's identity;
you would cheat us out of who God made you to be.
You are a treasure in the works . . . as yet, unfinished –
The Master is still forming and molding you.
Yield to Him, to His kind and gentle hands.
Cling to Him in times of hurt and doubt.
Be soothed by His words, which tear down every lie,
but build up truth.
Let God be your foundation upon which you are being built.
You will be a delight to the Lord . . .
and so you shall complete the gift you are to us all.

Jacqueline Marie Sparaco

It Pleased My Lord

It pleased my Lord when I received
mercies tender when I was grieved.
Snuggling in the splendor of His loving hold,
my trusting heart like flower petals that unfold.

It pleased my Lord, and I rejoiced to leave sin's evil snare.
Justice and mercy satisfied at the cross when Christ,
in my place, laid bare –
God's wrath diffused by Son's willing death.
What Extravagant love that takes away my breath!

It pleased my Lord to feed my soul,
heal my wounds, make me whole.
To burn all dross from filth and stain
by Holy fire in His Mighty Name.

It pleased my Lord to raise me up
and set my feet on a higher place –
dressed in His righteousness, love and grace,
with all bright countenance upon my face.

It pleased my Lord: my faith.
And I am thankful still
to follow Him for all my days and satisfy His will.
I can triumph over sullen paths, beyond the troubles I see . . .
because His unfailing love and grace are always there for me!

When Death Touched My Hand

Here lay a fragile sparrow
in the palm of my hand –
the hour of death upon her:
She sang no more a song,
her mouth closed tight,
not a fight left in her,
and she did not quiver.

In one motionless moment
her eyes were wide-opened.
They stared into mine as if knowing –
knowing what was coming.
It was then I saw her strength.

I prayed that death would pass her by,
A sadness gripped my heart.
Kissing her soft little head I knelt there helplessly.

Her eyelids weighed visibly heavily now,
her small body slumped in my palm.
I laid her down gently, turning away for a moment
as I looked up into the vast blue sky.
But when I returned my gaze to her,
she was gone, eyes closed, breath stopped, no motion . . .
No hint of life,
not a quiver or beat of the heart.
All life left my fragile little friend.
I carried her and buried her under a Weeping Willow.

Such a small and peaceful creature –
maybe the one who sang by my window every morning.

And the world continued, moving on
during this, her last hour.
God's precious little creation . . . I noted . . .
And death had touched my hand.

"Ghosts"

I see them! All around me!
Many pass them by without blinking or glancing.
I recognize the cloud of gray encompassing them. I recognize the pain.
Some smile only ever so slightly . . . while most avoid eye contact,
and move hastily away.

But their eyes give them away.
In my short life, I've seen through these "windows to the soul."
Yes, many are the eyes I've peered into:
laughing eyes, searching eyes, eyes contented,
eyes confused, and very angry eyes.
But in these "ghostly" eyes, there is distress:
great pain, grief, and longing.
They are frozen, and as in a deep, thick fog,
having no way forward and no way back,
they are lost.
Opaque are these ghosts. Not solid.
Not completely transparent.

I would take them by the hand to Jesus,
Who leads us to gardens where His love and peace reign.
Where He is, there are soothing sounds: of babbling brooks,
the fragrance of sweet flowers that glide upon gentle breezes;
here is where troubled and wounded souls find their consolation,
birds sing harmoniously, crickets chirp,
and everything gleams brightly
under the Care of the Great Shepherd.
For, where the Spirit and Presence of God is, there is freedom –
found in the calm deliverance and full healing!
And these "ghosts" are no longer "ghosts."
They are the living.

And the "world" rushing by them is gray, as walking dead.

The One, who is our Life Source, our Light of Life:
He brought us forth and He will lead us home.

For the Forsaken Ones . . .

Slowly dying, her tears are hot as they roll down her cheeks,
enflamed by scorn.
Her love, it's been trampled . . .
Her love, unacknowledged.
Like wax, does her heart melt within.
Her pulse wanes.
Her strength begins to fail.

She believes that love is always just out of reach.
Love appears unattainable to her.
She was told often that he "couldn't give her what he didn't have."

But God is Love!!!
Revive her Love!
Make her live again!

In her pain she asks "Is this just how it is for everyone?
Do we all starve for love?
Do we all have to face rejection?
Do we all falter in our steps?
Is there even a path that's steady and stable?"

She slumps to the floor and weeps:
My ankles are weak from all their twisting, straining, and stumbling!
My back fails from bearing heavy loads for so long!
My knees no longer support me!
They strain with each step, failing to hold me up!
My head, neck, and shoulders ache!
So much pressure encompasses her.
She feels her heart will implode!
And her eyes drown in their sorrow.

Her breath grows shallow and desperate.

Her hearing becomes duller from the pressure in her head.

Her arms are no longer dependable, but weak. Strength is gone!

"I'm nearly no more!" she cries!

"Does anyone hear? Does anyone see?"

See how she fades?!

Oh, to be the free-spirited child once again!

Believing! Trusting! Hoping!

Oh, to laugh so carelessly – free again!

Oh, that innocence would return to my thoughts?

No more guile or deceit. Just pureness of heart!

She longs for when things were simple, and she felt content.

She longs to feel safe again in God's swaddling love,

treasured and happy, forever in Him.

Give her an enduring spirit, for Jesus's sake,

And satisfy her with the bread from heaven!

And Living water!!!

Restore her, O' Lord!

You are the Healer, and You make all things new!

KINDNESS

I see a spark in you . . .
>> It ignites me . . .
>>> I feel the strength in you . . .
>>>> It invites me . . .
>>>>> to be strong, too!

I listen to your voice . . .
>> I am calmed . . .
>>> I am warmed . . .
>>>> I find solace in my storm.

When you smile . . .
>> the hard shell around my heart breaks . . .
>>> I'll face whatever it takes . . .
>>>> because I have hope again!

Thank you!
>> Thank you, true
>>> for just being you!
>>>> In my dark, in my doubt,
>>>>> I find myself anew!

Again, friend, again . . .
>> Thank you for your gift to me . . .
>>> kindness shown in my agony!

For Charnelle
(in memory of Jon)

My heart is overwhelmed in my chest.
My breath has been taken away.
My life is not mattering so much to me right now.
This is losing the treasure of one I love deeply!
My son . . .
taken away too soon . . . How? Why? I don't understand!

My heart is overwhelmed in my chest.
My breath has been taken away.
 My life is not mattering much to me.
This is gaining the treasure of Jesus,
Whom I love, and who loves me.
He gave Himself up for me!
How? Why? I don't understand!
He took away all my sin, and banished death and the grave.
I may not understand, but I believe and receive this gift.
And He holds my treasure in His arms until I go to him.
["I will go to him but he will not return to me. 2 Samuel 12:23"]

For Charnelle . . . with love.

Jesus Never Disappoints

Talk of Christmases gone by.
Expectations sure run high –
of things to give
and things to have.
The dreams and wishes make us sigh.

But you will never disappoint me, Jesus!
You could never leave me sad and bare.
Every gift under my Christmas tree
could never match Your love for me.
I have all I ever need in You.

Ribbon, bows, and wrap lay scattered.
Thoughts of those whose lives are tattered –
disappointing scenes are all around.
But even though these hearts seem shattered,
there is a hope that still is true:
There is no greater gift we have
at Christmastime than You.

For You will never disappoint us, Jesus.
You are all our lives are searching for.
And though we get distracted,
please draw us back to You.
No other gift at Christmastime could ever do.

You will never disappoint me, Jesus.
You are always faithful and true.
No one else has ever loved us
the way You always do.
Jesus, there is just no other
that can save us like You do!

Jacqueline Marie Sparaco

God's Perfect Package

There's a very special glimmer.
There's a very special glow.
That God in His abundant love,
wants you and me to know.

He wrapped a gift in swaddling clothes,
and sent Him to this Earth.
A very special woman, Mary,
with strong faith gave Him birth.

'Twas the Child of His favor –
the Perfect and Holy One.
The only Way, Truth, and Life . . .
this is God, the Son.

No greater love has anyone known –
that He took our punishment for our sin,
dying all alone.

The Father had to turn away –
the pain of such a sight!
But daybreak came back again
and chased away the night.
Christ rose from the grave;
He reigns in glorious light!

No more will man be separated because of daunting sin,
for Jesus's sacrifice has removed it,
allowing us access to go in.
There's nothing we can say or do
except believe what He says is true!

So celebrate this gift of love
while it is called "today."
As far as you could ever run,
this gift is never too far away!

This is My Meditation

My meditation takes me into a swirl of engaging thoughts:
The Lord has touched the still waters of my life,
making a rippled effect.
And other times, He has touched my stormy waves, making them still.
The motion of His Spirit catches my spiritual eye by surprise . . .
You are awesome, my Lord!
You know what I need and when I need it!
You have reached me through faithful believers,
mighty prayer warriors, and "doers" of the Word.
I see myself in the same position as your disciples
when they followed Jesus, before His death and resurrection –
feeling so scared and insecure, but captivated by Jesus,
His words and His actions.
Therefore, You astound me, Lord.
And You stir my heart and mind and soul.
A boldness grows within me.
I have been learning the mission, but often have missed the call . . .
there is so much to comprehend.
I see my feet tracing Christ's steps . . . to death.
The shadow of the cross falls over me.
My shadow is enveloped by His.
My heart trembles:
It is death to self, but life to my spirit – my life hidden in Him.
This empty shell of mine becomes filled
with the power of His Presence . . .
I am weak, but He is strong!
I am blind, but I can see through His eyes now.
I was lost, but I am found in Him.
"Bless the Lord O my soul!! And forget not His benefits –
who forgives all your sins, who heals all your diseases,
who redeems your life from the pit.

He crowns you with love and compassion,
He satisfies your desires with good things,
and your youth is renewed like the eagle's. [Psalm 103: 2-4]"
Praise the Lord!!